Looking at Countries

ISRAEL

Kathleen Pohl

W

FRANKLIN WATTS
LONDON·SYDNEY

This edition first published in 2008 by Franklin Watts

Franklin Watts
338 Euston Road
London NW1 3BH

Franklin Watts Australia
Level 17/207 Kent Street
Sydney, NSW 2000

First published in 2008 by Gareth Stevens Publishing
1 Reader's Digest Road
Pleasantville
NY 10570-7000 USA

ISBN: 978 0 7496 8246 0
Dewey number: 915.694

Senior Managing Editor: Lisa M. Guidone
Senior Editor: Barbara Bakowski
Creative Director: Lisa Donovan
Designer: Tammy West
Photo Researcher: Sylvia Ohlrich
Reading Consultant: Susan Nations, M.Ed.

Photo credits: (t=top, b=bottom)
Cover (main) Age Fotostock; cover (inset) Jon Arnold Images/SuperStock; title page Alberto Biscaro/Masterfile;
p. 4 Ohad Shahar/Alamy; p. 6 Richard Ashworth/Getty Images; p. 7t Sylvain Grandadam/Age Fotostock; p. 7b
D. Usher/Peter Arnold; p. 8 Haim Azulay/Reuters/Landov; p. 9t Duby Tal/Alamy; p. 9b Hanan Isachar/Corbis; p.
10 Gil Cohen Magen/Reuters/Landov; p. 11t Shutterstock; p. 11b Ammar Awad/Reuters/Landov; p. 12t Nayeff
Hashlamoun/Reuters/Landov; p. 12b Debbie Hill/UPI/Landov; p. 13 Gadi Geffen/Israel Images/Alamy; p. 14 Jon
Arnold Images/SuperStock; p. 15t Victor de Schwanberg/Alamy; p. 15b R. Matina/Age Fotostock; p. 16 George
Simhoni/Masterfile; p. 17t Niall Benvie/Corbis; p. 17b Jacky Costi/Alamy; p. 18 Israel Images/Alamy; p. 19t Israel
Images/Alamy; p. 19b Christine Osborne Pictures/Alamy; p. 20t Tim Hill/Alamy; p. 20b George
Simhoni/Masterfile; p. 21t Jon Arnold Images/SuperStock; p. 21b Richard Nowitz/Israel Images/Alamy; p. 22
Mark Boulton/Alamy; p. 23t David Silverman/Getty Images; p. 23b Israel Images/Alamy; p. 24 Cris Haigh/Getty
Images; p. 25t Eddie Gerald/Bloomberg/Landov; p. 25b Edi Israel/Israel Sun/Landov; p. 26 SuperStock; p. 27t
SuperStock; p. 27b Eitan Simanor/Alamy. Every attempt has been made to clear copyright. Should there be any
inadvertent omission please apply to the publisher for rectification.

Printed in China

Franklin Watts is a division of Hachette Children's Books, an Hachette Livre UK company.
www.hachettelivre.co.uk

Contents

Where is Israel?

Israel is in a part of the world called the Middle East. It shares borders with four other countries – Egypt to the south-west, Jordan and Syria to the east and Lebanon to the north. Israel is shaped like a long, thin arrow. It meets the Mediterranean Sea at the top and the Red Sea at the bottom.

Did you know?

Even though Israel is small, it includes deserts, mountains, valleys and coasts.

ASIA

EUROPE

ISRAEL

AFRICA

Israel is a small country in west Asia, in an area called the Middle East.

Israel's parliament is called the Knesset and it is in Jerusalem, the capital city.

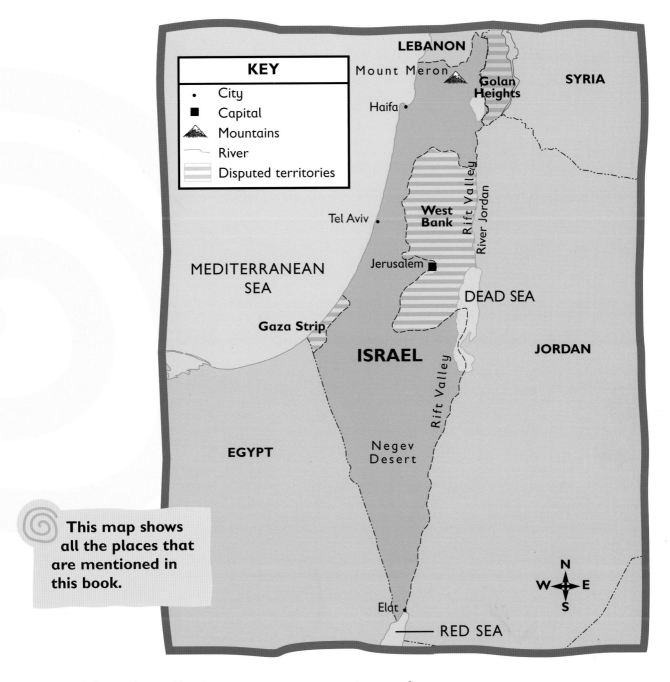

KEY

- • City
- ■ Capital
- ▲ Mountains
- ∿ River
- ▥ Disputed territories

LEBANON

Mount Meron

Golan Heights

SYRIA

Haifa

West Bank

Rift Valley

River Jordan

Tel Aviv

MEDITERRANEAN SEA

Jerusalem

DEAD SEA

Gaza Strip

JORDAN

ISRAEL

Rift Valley

EGYPT

Negev Desert

This map shows all the places that are mentioned in this book.

N
W E
S

Elat

RED SEA

Israel has hardly been at peace since the country was founded in 1948. When it became a Jewish state other people already lived there, particularly the Palestinians. This fact continues to cause problems in the area. Israel has also fought with nearby countries, particularly Lebanon, for control of important land areas.

The landscape

Most Israelis live in big cities on the flat area of land in the west of the country. Some of the land is good farming land and there are sandy beaches along the Mediterranean Sea.

The Rift Valley is a long strip of flat, low land in the east. The River Jordan, which flows through the valley, is Israel's longest river. It empties into the Dead Sea which is so salty that only a few plants and animals can live in it. The salt allows people to float very easily.

Did you know?

The shore of the Dead Sea is the lowest place on the Earth's surface.

The Dead Sea is really a saltwater lake. The salt forms strange shapes on the beach.

The Negev Desert has cliffs and canyons.

The Negev Desert in the south covers over half of Israel. Few people live in this hot, dry place although nomads have always lived there.

Mountains and hills make up most of northern and central Israel. The highest peak is Mount Meron, in the north.

Wild goats called ibex live in the desert mountains.

Weather and seasons

Even though Israel is a small country, the weather can be very different in the north and the south. It is almost always hot and dry in the south, where there is desert. However, snow can fall in the mountains of the north. Generally, the seasons follow the same pattern as ours although summers are much hotter.

Did you know?

In spring and autumn, Israel can suffer hot, dry winds from deserts in nearby countries.

Even though much of Israel is hot and dry, snow sometimes falls in the mountains.

With little rainfall, farmers have to water their crops.

Every year Israelis celebrate a special tree-planting holiday. The trees help to prevent the soil from blowing away.

The amount of rainfall varies a lot in different parts of the country. December is the rainiest month, especially in the northern hills. Thunderstorms are common.

The Negev Desert, in the south, is the driest area. Almost no rain falls there.

Israeli people

Almost seven million people live in Israel and most of them are Jewish. They follow the laws of Judaism, one of the world's oldest religions. Some Jews follow strict rules about when to pray, how to dress and what to eat. Others do not follow such strict rules.

Arabs live in Israel, too. Most Arabs are Muslim although a few are Christian. Israeli Arabs and Jews often try to keep apart, living in separate areas of a city and following different lifestyles and customs.

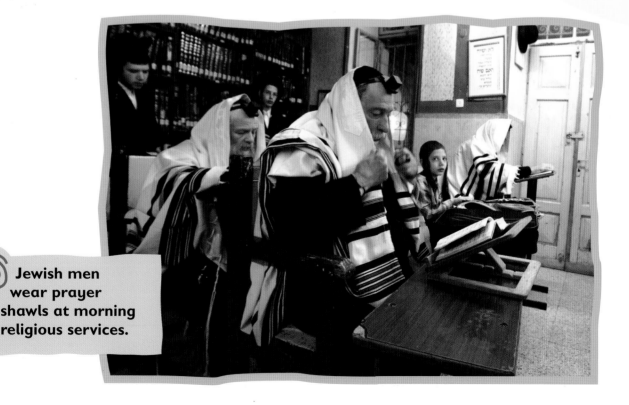

Jewish men wear prayer shawls at morning religious services.

Did you know?
Almost three million tourists visit Israel each year.

Signs are printed in Hebrew, Arabic and English.

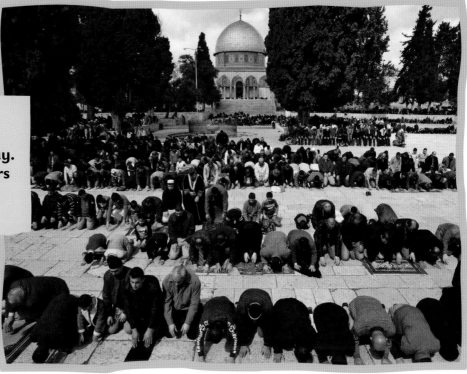

Muslims pray together on Fridays at midday. Some worshippers kneel on prayer mats.

Israel has two main languages, Hebrew and Arabic. Jewish people mostly speak Hebrew – Arabs mostly speak Arabic. Many people in Israel speak English, too.

School and family

Children attend school between the ages of five and sixteen. Almost all Muslim and Jewish children go to separate schools. Some schools are run by the government and some are religious schools.

Students learn maths, science, reading and art. They study Hebrew or Arabic and learn English, too. Children go to school six days a week.

Muslim girls and boys usually go to separate schools.

Children learn to use computers at school.

Did you know?

Muslim students do not go to school on Friday, because it is their holy day. Jewish students do not have school on Saturday, their holy day.

Children help with jobs around the house and on farms. This boy is carrying firewood.

A few Jewish and Arab students go to school together. They learn their lessons in both Arabic and Hebrew.

After school, many children play sport or take art or music lessons. At home, they help with chores. Most Jewish families are small, with two or three children. Arab families are usually bigger. About half of all Jewish women work outside the home while most Arab women do not.

Country

In the past, unlike today, many people in Israel lived in the countryside. Most people who live in the country today are farmers. Some live on a kibbutz, where people live and work together. They work on the kibbutz farm or in factories.

Members of a kibbutz share the land and the business. Instead of being paid money, they often get food, housing and schooling in exchange for work.

This photo, taken from the air, shows a large kibbutz.

Children on a kibbutz share the work, including caring for farm animals.

Did you know?

In the past, children on a kibbutz lived in a separate children's house. They spent just a few hours a day with their parents.

About one-third of Israel's farm goods are grown on kibbutzim.

Families live in separate houses on the kibbutz but everyone gathers to eat meals together in a big dining room.

Israeli farmers grow cereal crops, cotton, fruit – including oranges and lemons, and vegetables. They also raise goats, sheep, cows and chickens.

City

Most people in Israel live and work in cities. Jerusalem, the capital, is the biggest city. Many of its streets are crowded with cars and buses. Parts of Jerusalem have new shopping centres and modern office buildings. In older areas, outdoor markets line stone streets.

Did you know?

Jerusalem is sometimes called 'the City of Gold'. Many buildings are built from a pink-white stone that looks golden in the sunshine.

A shopping street in Jerusalem.

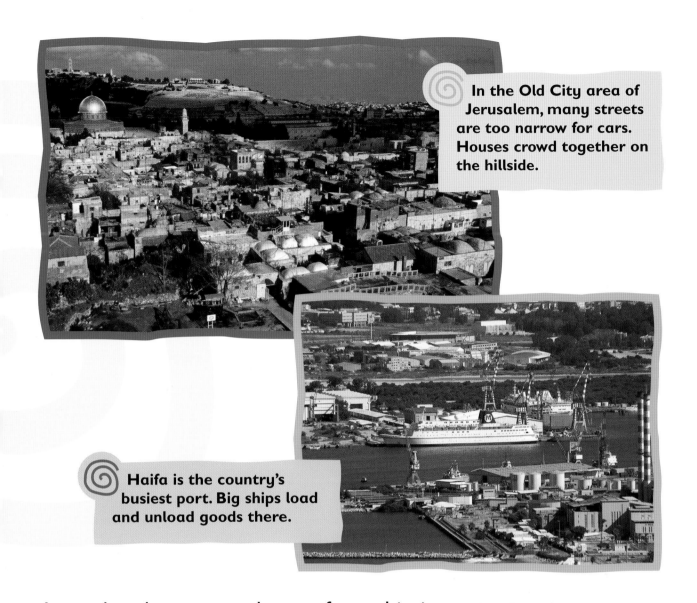

In the Old City area of Jerusalem, many streets are too narrow for cars. Houses crowd together on the hillside.

Haifa is the country's busiest port. Big ships load and unload goods there.

Jerusalem has many places of worship important to people of different religions. Jews, Muslims and Christians from all over the world travel to Israel to visit them.

The second-biggest city is Tel Aviv, a modern city. It has tall buildings, cafés, beaches and museums. It is an important business centre. Haifa is a major port on the coast of the Mediterranean Sea. Elat is a busy port on the Red Sea and has beautiful beaches.

Israeli homes

In the cities, most people live in small flats in apartment blocks. They are usually made of stone, and many have a balcony. In hot weather, people sometimes eat outside on their balcony to try to keep cool.

Did you know?

Almost all households in Israel have a mobile phone.

Many people live in high-rise apartment blocks in Israel's large cities.

People on a kibbutz live in small houses. The homes have white walls and red tile roofs. Some rich people in Israel live in large houses and apartments.

In the desert, nomadic Bedouins move from place to place, caring for their sheep and goats. Bedouins take their tents with them when they move on in search of grazing land. Some Bedouins have settled in villages as it is difficult to live their traditional life.

Food

People have come from many countries to live in Israel. They eat all sorts of foods. Falafel is a favourite Middle Eastern dish. It is fried chickpeas with spices.

People in Israel eat a lot of rice, fruit and vegetables. Eggs, cheese and bread are popular, too. Some people enjoy salad for breakfast. Lunch is usually the main meal of the day.

Falafel in pitta bread, is a popular dish. Pitta is a thin, flat bread made into a pocket.

Markets sell dried fruits grown by Israeli farmers.

People like eating in restaurants and cafés in Israel's cities.

Jewish families celebrate religious festivals with special prayers and food.

Many Jewish people follow strict rules about food. For example, they do not eat pork. They follow Jewish food laws to prepare meals that are kosher. Most restaurants and hotels in Israel serve kosher food.

Did you know?

During the Jewish holiday of Passover, Jews eat a kind of bread called matzo. It is flat, like a cracker.

At work

Many people in Israeli cities work in banks, hotels and shops. Some people are teachers, doctors or nurses, others write for newspapers or work for the government. Israeli scientists work to help people stay healthy. Others find new ways to move water to dry areas so that farmers can grow food.

Some people work in factories. They make products such as paper, chemicals, electrical and plastic goods, as well as clothing. Miners get salt and other minerals from the Dead Sea.

Workers remove salt from the Dead Sea. It is the world's saltiest lake.

Most of the world's diamonds pass through Israel. Workers there cut and polish the rough stones. Then they sell the cut diamonds to people around the world.

Most young Israelis are expected to do military service in the army, navy or airforce. They sign on at the age of 18. Men must serve for three years and women for about two years.

Did you know?
Israel sells more cut diamonds than any other country.

This worker looks closely at a cut diamond.

Female soldiers train to serve in Israel's army. Men and women are trained to use guns.

Having fun

Israel has many attractive beaches on its long coastline. Swimming, sailing and windsurfing are popular activities. People also enjoy beach volleyball and matkot, a beach tennis game.

Many people like team sports, too. They play and watch football and basketball. Every four years, Jewish athletes from around the world come to Israel for the Maccabiah Games.

Many people in Israel enjoy the country's beautiful beaches.

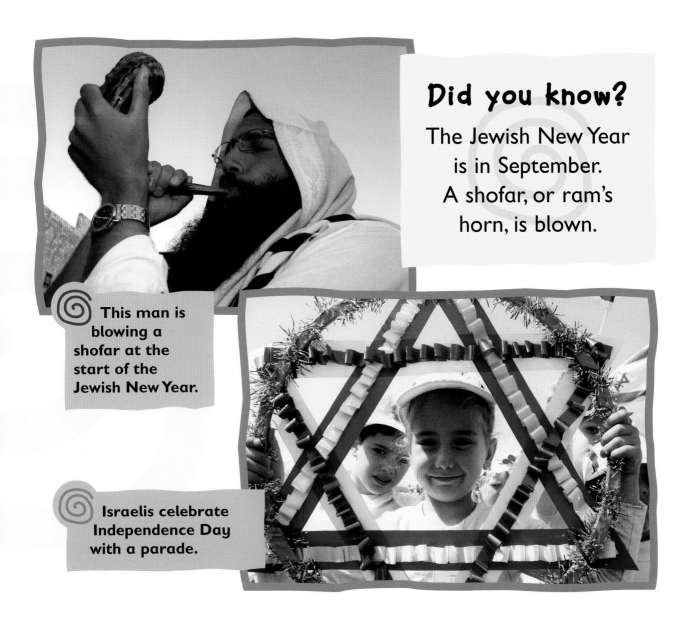

This man is blowing a shofar at the start of the Jewish New Year.

Israelis celebrate Independence Day with a parade.

Israelis enjoy the arts – they read, visit museums and go to theatres and concerts. Israelis also enjoy playing and listening to music and dancing. Most children and teenagers join youth groups. There they enjoy picnics, plays and other fun events and learn more about their country.

Jews, Muslims and Christians celebrate religious holidays in special ways throughout the year.

Israel: the facts

- The official name of Israel is the State of Israel.

- Israel is a democracy. The people vote to elect government leaders.

- The Knesset is the Israeli parliament. It has 120 elected members. The president has formal duties. The prime minister handles the day-to-day business of running the government.

- All citizens who are 18 or older may vote in elections.

- Hebrew and Arabic are the languages of Israel.

The flag of Israel shows a blue Star of David in the middle. The star is a very old Jewish symbol.

The Israeli unit of money is the shekel.

Did you know?

In biblical times, the shekel was a unit of measurement – a set amount of barley.

Jewish families celebrate Hanukkah, a festival of lights held in December.

Glossary

Bedouin nomadic people who have lived in the Negev Desert for thousands of years.

Christianity the religion of Christians, based on the life and teachings of Jesus Christ.

Customs traditions or usual ways of acting in a community or group.

Democracy a government elected by the people of a country.

Factories a building or group of buildings where goods are made.

Falafel a popular Middle Eastern food made of fried chickpeas and spices.

Graze to put animals out to eat grass.

Islam the religion of Muslims, who worship Allah.

Judaism the religion of the Jews, based on the Torah, the Jewish holy book.

Kibbutz (plural: kibbutzim) a farm or settlement in Israel where people live and work together.

Knesset the parliament where the Israeli government meets to make laws and run the country.

Kosher foods that are prepared following Jewish food laws.

Matkot a beach tennis game played in Israel.

Matzo a flat bread eaten during Passover, a Jewish holiday.

Minerals solid materials mined or dug from the ground, such as coal and diamonds.

Nomads people who wander from place to place, living in tents and grazing their animals.

Pitta a thin, flat bread folded into a pocket.

Port a town or city where goods are brought in and sent out on ships.

Shekel the basic unit of money, or currency, in Israel.

Shofar a ram's-horn trumpet blown during some Jewish holidays.

Find out more

http://news.bbc.co.uk/cbbcnews/hi/guides/default.stm
Visit this site for Newsround guides on Israel and neighbouring countries, as well as one on religious festivals, including Jewish festivals.

www.woodlandsjunior.kent.sch.uk/Homework/religion/jewish.htm
Woodland Junior School's informative website about Judaism.

Note to parents and teachers: Every effort has been made by the Publishers to ensure that these websites are suitable for children, that they are of the highest educational value, and that they contain no inappropriate or offensive material. However, because of the nature of the Internet, it is impossible to guarantee that the contents of these sites will not be altered. We strongly advise that Internet access is supervised by a responsible adult.

Hebrew and Arabic

Hebrew and Arabic are the main languages used in Israel. Both languages use different alphabets to our own. You can learn how to say a few words of Hebrew below.

English word	Hebrew word
hello/peace	shalom
yes	ken
no	lo
good	tov
good morning	boker tov
thank you	tola
please	bevakasha

You may know more Arabic than you think! Some Arabic words have found their way into English. Here are a few of them:

lime orange sofa mosque lake giraffe guitar monsoon

My map of Israel

Trace this map, colour it in and use the map on page 5 to write the names of all the towns.

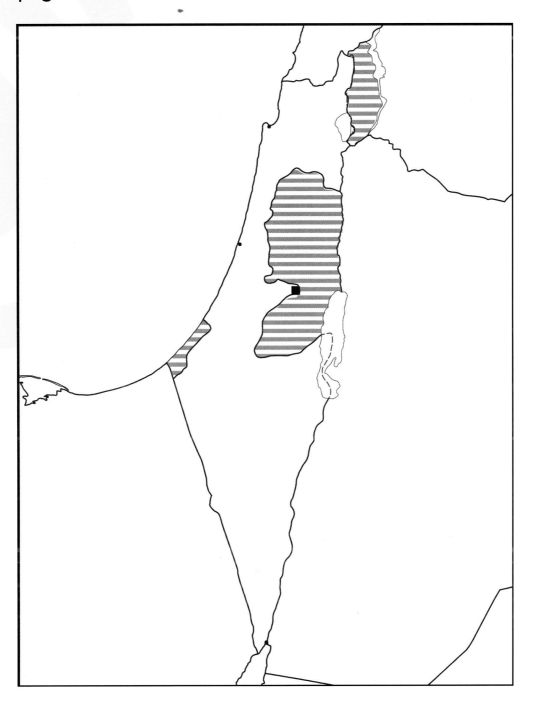

Index